Grade 2

Writer's Handbook

KENDALL/HUNT PUBLISHING COMPANY
Dubuque, Iowa

AUTHOR TEAM

Terry Heinecke	Jean Sherlock
Kim O'Brien	Sandra McEowen
Joyce Bieber	Pam Vincent

THE WRITER'S HANDBOOK
Grade Two
Table of Contents

Dear Student,

This *Writer's Handbook* is a special book just for you. As you begin to write, use this book to help you put your ideas on paper.

You will find many helpful words in this book. There are color words, number words, and words that tell about some of the special days of the year. There are words that mean almost the same as another word as well as words that mean the opposite. This book also has a dictionary with words second graders like to use when they write.

If you want to write a story, this book will help you get started. It will also show you how to publish a story. Use this *Writer's Handbook* to help you become a real author.

ABC Order

The order of letters from A to Z is called ABC order (alphabetical order). ABC order always stays the same. Listed below are the letters of the alphabet in ABC order.

a b c d e f g h i j k l m n o p q r s t u v w x y z
A B C D E F G H I J K L M N O P Q R S T U V W X Y Z

MIXED LETTERS	ABC ORDER
c a b	a b c
f e d	d e f
t r s	r s t
x z y	x y z

Words can be put into ABC order. Words in the dictionary are in ABC order. Use the first letter of each word to put it in ABC order. Listed below are some words in ABC order.

ant	fin	let	rat
bug	goat	man	sun
cat	happy	net	tree

When words begin with the same letter, use the second letter to put them in ABC order. Listed below are words that are also in ABC order.

gate	lion	story
gift	lunch	water
great	school	wet
leg	sleep	white

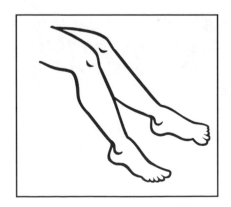

Dictionary

The words listed below are the most commonly used words in writing. They are also the most frequently misspelled words.

Aa

a	ago	an	as
able	ahead	any	ashes
about	air	anyhow	ask
above	airport	anyone	asking
act	alike	anything	at
add	alive	apple	aunt
added	all	are	author
adding	almost	arm	away
after	along	army	
afternoon	also	around	
age	always	art	

Bb

babies	bats	bell	blue
back	battle	belong	boat
bad	bay	belongs	boats
bags	be	belt	body
bake	bean	bent	bone
baked	became	beside	bother
band	because	best	box
bank	become	better	brand
banker	becomes	big	brave
banking	bedroom	bill	bread
banks	bedtime	black	bright
bark	bee	blank	bring
baseball	been	block	brings
bass	before	blood	broke
bat	behind	blow	brother
bath	being	blowing	brown

bud   bunch   butter   by

bugs   but   buy

_____

_____ 2

_____

_____

_____

_____

_____

_____

_____

_____

_____

Cc

cake	chair	colder
cakes	chalk	color
call	change	come
called	chapter	comes
calls	charge	coming
came	church	cone
can	circus	content
candy	city	contest
cans	class	cook
cap	clean	cooked
caps	clear	cooking
card	clerk	cool
care	clock	copyright
cart	closet	cord
case	club	corn
cave	clubs	could
cent	coat	count

cover   cross   cups

covering   crossing   cut

cream   cry

crop   cup

_____

_____

_____

_____

_____

_____

_____

_____

Dd

dad	dear	dinner	draw
daddy	dedicated	discount	dream
dance	deer	dish	drink
danger	depart	display	drive
dark	department	do	drop
date	desk	dogs	drove
dated	did	doing	drum
daughter	died	done	dry
day	dig	doors	dust
deal	dime	down	

_____

_____

_____

_____

_____

Ee

each	eating	even
ear	eats	every
earth	eggs	everyone
east	eight	export
eat	end	

Ff

face	feel	flag	forgot
fall	feet	floor	form
falling	fight	flow	fort
farm	file	flowers	found
farmer	fill	fly	four
farms	finding	food	fox
fast	fine	foods	Friday
faster	fire	fool	frog
fat	fish	foot	from
father	fished	for	full
fee	fishing	forever	fully
feed	fix	forget	fun

_____

_____

_____

_____

Gg

game	given	good	great
games	gives	goods	green
garden	glad	goose	group
gas	glass	got	grove
gate	go	grade	grow
gave	goal	grain	grown
get	goat	grandfather	gum
gets	goats	grandmother	gun
getting	goes	grant	guns
gift	going	grass	
girl	gone	grave	

Hh

had	have	high	hope
hair	having	hill	hopes
half	hay	hills	horn
hall	he	him	horse
ham	head	himself	horses
hammer	headed	his	hot
hand	hear	history	hour
handed	heater	hit	hours
hands	help	hits	houses
happy	helping	holding	how
hard	helps	hole	hunt
harm	her	home	hunter
has	here	homes	hunting
hate	hers	hop	

Ii

I	illustrated	income	into
if	in	ink	is
ill	inch	inside	it

_____

_____

_____

_____

_____

_____

_____

_____

_____

Jj

job   joy   jumps

joke   jump   just

Kk

keep   kill   kind   kitten

keeping   killed   kindly   knife

key   killing   king   know

2

_____

_____

_____

_____

_____

_____

_____

_____

_____

Ll

lake	laws	life	long
lamp	lay	light	longer
land	laying	like	looked
landing	leader	line	lost
lands	leading	lines	lot
lap	learn	lions	loved
lard	leave	lip	lovely
large	leaves	list	low
larger	leaving	listed	luck
largest	left	little	lumber
last	leg	live	lunch
lasted	less	lived	
late	let	lives	
law	letter	lock	

_____

_____

_____

Mm

mad	market	missing	mouth
made	may	mom	move
mail	me	mommy	moved
make	mean	Monday	much
makes	meat	money	mud
many	mile	moon	must
map	milk	more	my
maps	milking	most	myself
march	mind	motel	
mark	miss	mother	

Nn

nail	need	nine	note
name	nest	no	notes
named	net	nobody	nothing
names	never	noise	now
nation	new	noon	numbers
near	next	north	nut
nearly	nice	nose	
neck	night	not	

_____

_____

_____

_____

_____

_____

Oo

object	on	or	outline
of	once	orange	outside
off	one	order	over
oil	only	other	overcome
older	open	our	
oldest	opens	out	

Pp

pack	payment	plant
packing	payments	planted
page	peach	plate
pages	pen	play
paint	penny	played
pal	people	player
pan	person	playing
paper	phone	please
park	pick	plow
part	pie	point
parts	pies	points
party	pilot	pony
pass	pine	pool
passing	pink	poor
path	pipe	port
pay	place	post
paying	placed	posted

pound	protest	push
pounds	published	put
pray	pull	puts
price	purple	

2

_____

_____

_____

_____

_____

_____

_____

_____

_____

_____

Qq

quack   queen   quilt

Rr

race	reader	return	rooms
rail	reading	reward	root
railroad	ready	rich	rope
rain	real	ride	rose
rained	rear	rides	roses
raining	recover	right	row
rains	red	ring	rub
ranch	rent	rings	rug
rang	rented	river	rule
range	reported	road	rush
rate	rest	rocks	
read	rested	rode	

Ss

sad	schoolhouse	shoe	sit
said	schools	shop	six
sail	scout	short	sixteen
sailing	sea	should	sky
salt	seat	show	sled
same	see	showed	sleep
sand	seed	showing	slow
sane	seeds	sick	small
sang	seen	side	smoke
sat	self	sides	snow
Saturday	send	silk	snowball
save	sent	sin	snowing
saved	seven	sing	snowman
saving	she	singer	so
saw	sheep	singing	soil
say	ship	sir	sold
school	shipment	sister	some

someone	spelling	staying	suffer
something	sport	stays	suit
sometime	spot	still	summer
son	spring	stop	sun
song	stamp	store	Sunday
soon	stand	story	sunlight
sound	standing	stove	sunshine
south	star	streets	supper
space	started	string	sweet
speed	state	student	
spell	stay	such	

_____

_____

_____

_____

_____

_____

Tt

table	tent	tip
take	tenth	tire
taken	test	title
takes	than	to
talk	thank	today
talking	that	toe
tall	the	told
tan	them	tomorrow
tank	there	ton
tar	they	tonight
tax	thing	took
tea	things	tooth
teach	think	top
teacher	this	tops
teachers	Thursday	town
teaching	time	towns
tell	times	toy

trade	trip	Tuesday
train	truck	turn
trains	true	twin
tree	trust	two
trees	try	

2

_____

_____

_____

_____

_____

_____

_____

_____

_____

Uu

unable	unlike	use
uncle	up	used
under	upon	
understand	us	

_____

_____

_____

_____

_____

_____

_____

_____

_____

Vv

vase   very   vote   voted

2

Ww

walk	Wednesday	white	without
walking	week	who	wood
walks	well	why	woods
wall	went	wife	wool
want	were	will	word
wanted	western	willing	work
war	wet	win	worked
was	what	wind	workers
wash	whatever	window	working
washed	wheat	wine	world
washing	when	wing	would
water	whenever	winter	
way	where	wish	
we	which	with	

_____

_____

_____

Xx

x-ray   xylem   xylophone

_____

_____

_____

_____

_____

_____

_____

_____

_____

_____

_____

Yy

yard	yell	yesterday	young
yards	yellow	yet	your
years	yes	you	yours

_____

_____

_____

_____

_____

_____

_____

_____

_____

_____

Zz

zero   zone   zoo

_____

_____

_____

_____

_____

_____

_____

_____

_____

_____

_____

_____

Word Lists

Abbreviations

An abbreviation is a short way to write a word.

apartment → apt.

avenue → Ave.

building → bldg.

company → co.

doctor → Dr.

dozen → doz.

drive → dr.

east → E

example → ex.

foot or feet → ft.

gallon → gal.

hour → hr.

illustration → illus.

inch → in.

medium → med.

midnight—
before noon → a.m./A.M.

miles per hour → mph

minute → min.

miscellaneous → misc.

misses → Mrs.

mister → Mr.

month → mo.

noon—
before midnight → p.m./P.M.

north → N

northeast → NE

northwest → NW

number → no.

ounce → oz.

package → pkg.

page	→ p./pg.	señor	→ Sr.
pages	→ pp.	señora	→ Sra.
paid	→ pd.	señorita	→ Srta.
pint	→ pt.	south	→ S
post office	→ P.O.	southeast	→ SE
pound	→ lb.	southwest	→ SW
president	→ pres.	square	→ sq.
principal	→ prin.	street	→ St.
quart	→ qt.	weight	→ wt.
road	→ Rd.	west	→ W
seconds	→ sec.	year	→ yr.

Antonyms

An antonym is a word that is opposite in meaning to another word.

add	→	subtract, decrease
afraid	→	bold, fearless, confident
angry	→	calm, pleasant
answer	→	question, ask
ask	→	answer, demand
awful	→	wonderful, fine
bad	→	good, marvelous
beautiful	→	homely, unattractive
bent	→	straight, unbent
big	→	little, small, tiny
boring	→	exciting, thrilling
brave	→	timid, scared, frightened
break	→	repair, mend, fix
bright	→	dim, dark, dull
careful	→	careless, thoughtless
catch	→	miss, free
clean	→	dirty, filthy

3

cold	→	hot, boiling
come	→	leave, depart
cry	→	laugh, giggle
cut	→	mend, repair
cute	→	disgusting, ugly
dangerous	→	safe, harmless
dark	→	light, bright
destroy	→	create, build
dirty	→	clean, pure
eat	→	starve, fast
end	→	beginning
enjoy	→	dislike, despise
excited	→	calm, quiet
exciting	→	boring, dull, uninteresting
explain	→	confuse, puzzle
fair	→	unjust, unfair
fall	→	rise, climb
fast	→	slow, unhurried, poky
fat	→	thin, slim, slender

find	→	lose, hide
friend	→	enemy, foe
get	→	give, lose
go	→	stop, stay, arrive
good	→	bad, naughty
great	→	small, little, awful
happy	→	sad, sorrowful
hard	→	simple, soft
hate	→	love, enjoy
have	→	need
help	→	harm, hurt
hide	→	uncover, discover
hold	→	release, drop
hot	→	cold, icy
hurry	→	delay, dawdle
hurt	→	help, comfort, heal
important	→	unimportant, trivial
interesting	→	boring, dull
keep	→	lose, misplace

3

kind	→	cruel, mean
large	→	small, tiny, little
laugh	→	cry, sob, weep
lazy	→	active, energetic
like	→	dislike, hate
little	→	big, large, bulky
loud	→	quiet, still, silent
love	→	hate, detest
mad	→	calm, quiet
make	→	break, destroy
mean	→	kind, gentle
move	→	remain, stay
neat	→	untidy, dirty, filthy
new	→	old, aged, ancient
old	→	new, recent, young
part	→	whole, total
place	→	remove, take
popular	→	unknown, unfamiliar
pretty	→	plain, ugly

pull	→	push, shove
push	→	pull, tug
quiet	→	loud, noisy, racket
right	→	wrong, incorrect, false, left
run	→	remain, stay
sad	→	happy, cheerful, glad
scared	→	bold, confident
shout	→	whisper, murmur
slow	→	fast, rapid, swift
smart	→	stupid, dull, dumb
smooth	→	rough, bumpy, uneven
soft	→	hard, rough
stop	→	go, start, begin
strange	→	ordinary, common
strong	→	weak, frail, flimsy
stupid	→	smart, bright, clever
sure	→	unsure, uncertain
take	→	leave
talk	→	hush, silent

3

thin	→	fat, thick
throw	→	catch, receive
ugly	→	beautiful, pretty, handsome
unhappy	→	happy, glad, delighted
wait	→	leave, hurry
walk	→	run
wet	→	dry, parched
worry	→	confident
wrong	→	right, correct, accurate

Color Words

This is how to spell some color words.

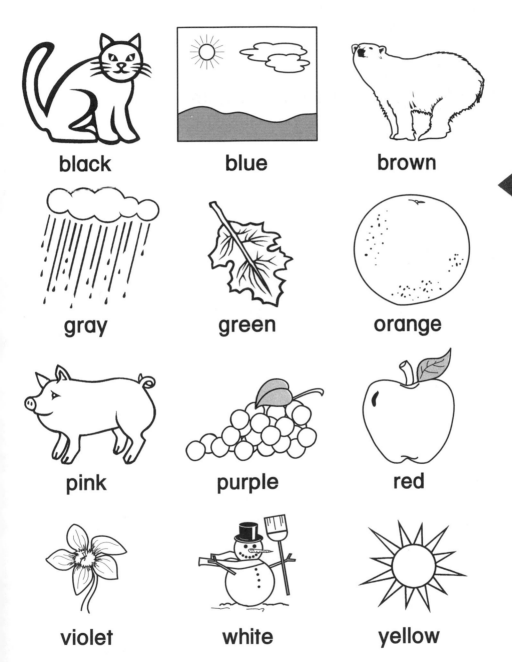

black   blue   brown

gray   green   orange

pink   purple   red

violet   white   yellow

3

Compound Words

A compound word is when two complete or whole words are put together to make a new word. Compound words are written together as one word with no spacing between them.

Example: bed + room = bedroom
out + side = outside

Listed below are some compound words.

afternoon	flashlight	playmate
airplane	football	railroad
baseball	inside	raincoat
birthday	into	rattlesnake
blueberry	ladybug	scrapbook
butterfly	lighthouse	something
countryside	lunchroom	sunshine
cowboy	mailman	today
doghouse	nickname	treetop
everyday	nighttime	underground
fireman	playground	wallpaper

Contractions

A contraction is a way to put two words together. An apostrophe takes the place of the letter or letters that are left out.

aren't	→	are not
can't	→	cannot
couldn't	→	could not
didn't	→	did not
doesn't	→	does not
don't	→	do not
hadn't	→	had not
hasn't	→	has not
haven't	→	have not
he'd	→	he would
he'll	→	he will
he's	→	he is
here's	→	here is
I'd	→	I would
I'll	→	I will
I'm	→	I am

3

I've	→	I have
isn't	→	is not
it'll	→	it will
it's	→	it is
let's	→	let us
she'd	→	she would
she'll	→	she will
she's	→	she is
shouldn't	→	should not
that's	→	that is
there's	→	there is
they'd	→	they would
they'll	→	they will
they're	→	they are
they've	→	they have
wasn't	→	was not
we'd	→	we would
we'll	→	we will
we're	→	we are

we've	→	we have
weren't	→	were not
what's	→	what is
who's	→	who is
won't	→	will not
wouldn't	→	would not
you'd	→	you would
you'll	→	you will
you're	→	you are
you've	→	you have

3

Days of the Week, Months of the Year

The days of the week and the months of the year can be written as a whole word or as an abbreviation. The whole word and the abbreviation begin with a capital letter. The abbreviation ends with a period.

Days and their abbreviations

Sunday	→	Sun.
Monday	→	Mon.
Tuesday	→	Tues.
Wednesday	→	Wed.
Thursday	→	Thurs.
Friday	→	Fri.
Saturday	→	Sat.

Months and their abbreviations

(Short months do not have abbreviations.)

January	→	Jan.
February	→	Feb.
March	→	Mar.
April	→	Apr.
May	→	May
June	→	June
July	→	July
August	→	Aug.
September	→	Sept.
October	→	Oct.
November	→	Nov.
December	→	Dec.

3

Holidays

Listed below are some of the special days of the year. Capitalize the important words in holidays.

New Year's Day	Memorial Day
Martin Luther King, Jr. Day	Flag Day
Lincoln's Birthday	Fourth of July
Valentine's Day	Labor Day
Washington's Birthday	Columbus Day
St. Patrick's Day	Halloween
Easter	Veteran's Day
Earth Day	Thanksgiving
Arbor Day	Hanukkah
May Day	Christmas

Homophones

Homophones are words that sound the same but have different spellings and different meanings.

ate	I ate my cookie with lunch.
eight	I will soon be eight years old.
bare	He likes to walk around in his bare feet.
bear	We saw a bear at the zoo.
be	I would like to be a pilot when I grow up.
bee	He was stung by a bee.
beat	Our team beat the other team in baseball.
beet	I had a beet on my plate for dinner.
blew	The wind blew all night.
blue	The sky is very blue today.
brake	I use the brake to stop my bike.
break	Don't break the dish.
buy	I will buy milk at the store.
by	We drove by your house.

3

dear	My dear friend is coming to dinner.
deer	We saw deer in the forest.
flew	The kite flew high in the sky.
flu	I am sick with the flu.
for	This book is for you to read.
four	My brother is four years old.
hair	I will comb my hair.
hare	The hare ran quickly across the yard.
hear	I can hear the baby crying.
here	Come here and look at my picture.
hole	I have a hole in my sock.
whole	I ate the whole apple.
hour	The movie will start in one hour.
our	This is our house.
it's	It's going to be a nice day.
its	The dog has its bone.

knew	I knew all the spelling words.
new	This fall I am going to a new school.
knight	The knight rode his horse to the castle.
night	We slept outside last night.
know	I know how to swim.
no	No, I don't want you to go home.
meat	We need to buy some meat at the store.
meet	I would like you to meet my new friend.
one	I am missing one of my shoes.
won	Our team won the soccer game.
pair	My pair of mittens are missing.
pear	I ate a big, juicy pear for lunch.
plain	I like my hamburgers plain.
	A plain is flat land with few trees.
plane	The plane flew over my house.
read	I read that book last night.
red	My favorite color is red.

3

right	I throw the ball with my right hand.
	She got that math problem right.
write	I am going to write my friend a letter.
road	The road was very bumpy.
rode	We rode our bikes after school.
sail	We sail on the lake.
sale	The store was having a sale.
sea	We went swimming in the sea.
see	I would like to see your picture.
sew	I will sew these pants for you.
so	I like you so much.
	The movie was over, so we all went home.
some	I need some paper.
sum	The sum of two plus two is four.
son	I took my son to the pool.
sun	The sun is bright today.

tail	The dog's tail is short and stubby.
tale	My teacher told the tale about Cinderella.
their	This is their cat.
there	The paper is over there.
they're	They're going to the movie soon.
threw	My friend threw the ball to me.
through	The bird flew through the window.
	I am through with my work.
to	I like going to school.
too	She would like an apple, too.
two	I have two pets at home.
weak	The flu made him weak and tired.
week	School starts this week.
wood	We need wood for the fire.
would	He would like to meet you.
you're	You're growing up so fast.
your	The dog has your shoe.

3

Number Words

Numbers can be written as a numeral or as a word.

0	zero	15	fifteen
1	one	16	sixteen
2	two	17	seventeen
3	three	18	eighteen
4	four	19	nineteen
5	five	20	twenty
6	six	30	thirty
7	seven	40	forty
8	eight	50	fifty
9	nine	60	sixty
10	ten	70	seventy
11	eleven	80	eighty
12	twelve	90	ninety
13	thirteen	100	one hundred
14	fourteen		

Signal Words

again	later
also	most of all
another	once
at last	one
but	other
finally	second
first	still
first of all	then
for one thing	third
last of all	

3

States/Abbreviations

Each state is followed by its abbreviation. The two letter abbreviation is always capitalized and does not end with a period.

Alabama	→	AL
Alaska	→	AK
Arizona	→	AZ
Arkansas	→	AR
California	→	CA
Colorado	→	CO
Connecticut	→	CT
Delaware	→	DE
Florida	→	FL
Georgia	→	GA
Hawaii	→	HI
Idaho	→	ID
Illinois	→	IL
Indiana	→	IN
Iowa	→	IA
Kansas	→	KS

Kentucky	→	KY
Louisiana	→	LA
Maine	→	ME
Maryland	→	MD
Massachusetts	→	MA
Michigan	→	MI
Minnesota	→	MN
Mississippi	→	MS
Missouri	→	MO
Montana	→	MT
Nebraska	→	NE
Nevada	→	NV
New Hampshire	→	NH
New Jersey	→	NJ
New Mexico	→	NM
New York	→	NY
North Carolina	→	NC
North Dakota	→	ND
Ohio	→	OH

3

Oklahoma	→	OK
Oregon	→	OR
Pennsylvania	→	PA
Rhode Island	→	RI
South Carolina	→	SC
South Dakota	→	SD
Tennessee	→	TN
Texas	→	TX
Utah	→	UT
Vermont	→	VT
Virginia	→	VA
Washington	→	WA
West Virginia	→	WV
Wisconsin	→	WI
Wyoming	→	WY

Syllables

A **syllable** is one or more letters in a word. A syllable always has a vowel and can be spoken by itself as a part of a word.

daddy = dad dy   sister = sis ter   baby = ba by

Dividing words into syllables

1. A one syllable word is never divided.

   boat   house   car   girl

2. Divide a compound word between the two words.

   pancake = pan cake

   bedroom = bed room

   into = in to

3. When a word begins with a prefix, divide the word between the prefix and the root/base word.

   unsold = un sold

   rewrite = re write

3

When a word ends with a suffix, divide the word between the suffix and the root/base word.

hopeless = hope less

careful = care ful

5. When two consonants come between two vowels in a word, divide between the two consonants.

ladder = lad der

swimming = swim ming

rescue = res cue

6. When one consonant comes between two vowels in a word and the first vowel is short, divide after the consonant.

lemon = lem on

river = riv er

travel = trav el

7. When one consonant comes between two vowels in a word and the first vowel is long, divide before the consonant.

tulip = tu lip

music = mu sic

bacon = ba con

Prefix

A prefix is a group of letters added to the beginning of a word that will change the word's meaning.

The baby was happy.

The baby was unhappy.

Prefix		Meaning		Example
re	→	again	→	rewrite
un	→	not	→	unhappy
dis	→	not	→	dislike

3

Suffix

A suffix is a group of letters added to the end of a word that will change the word's meaning.

We did not find a bone in the fish.

The fish was boneless.

Suffix	Meaning	Example
able	able to be	drinkable
ed	in the past	cooked
er	comparing two/ one who is	faster banker
es	more than one	dresses
est	comparing two or more	biggest
ful	full of	careful
ing	in the present	running
less	without	hopeless
ly	how	slowly
s	more than one	girls

Spelling rules for adding a suffix

1. When a root/base word has one vowel and the vowel is followed by one consonant, double the consonant if the suffix begins with a vowel.

   step + ed = stepped   run + er = runner

   big + est = biggest   skip + ing = skipping

2. When a root/base word ends with a silent *e*, drop the *e* if the suffix begins with a vowel.

   rake + ed = raked   write + er = writer

   large + est = largest   love + ing = loving

3. When a root/base word ends with a silent *e*, keep the *e* if the suffix begins with a consonant.

   home + less = homeless   use + ful = useful

4. When a root/base word ends with *y* and the *y* follows a consonant, change the *y* to *i* before adding the suffix.

   try + ed = tried   fly + er = flier

   hurry + es = hurries   funny + est = funniest

5. When a root/base word ends with *y* and the *y* follows a consonant, keep the *y* if the suffix begins with an *i*.

   try + ing = trying   hurry + ing = hurrying

3

Synonyms

A synonym is a word that has almost the same meaning as another word.

afraid	→	alarmed, frightened, scared, terrified
after	→	behind, following
all	→	entire, every
amazing	→	astonishing, incredible, unbelievable
angry	→	cross, furious
answer	→	reply, respond
ask	→	inquire, question, request
awful	→	dreadful, horrible, terrible
baby	→	infant, toddler
bad	→	evil, naughty, wicked
begin	→	commence, launch, start
below	→	beneath, under
big	→	enormous, gigantic, huge, tremendous
bite	→	chew, gobble, nibble
boring	→	dull, tiresome, uninteresting
boy	→	lad, youth

brave	→	bold, courageous, heroic
break	→	fracture, shatter, smash
bright	→	brilliant, gleaming, sparkling
buy	→	purchase
call	→	holler, scream, shout, yell
car	→	automobile, vehicle
carry	→	lug, tote, transport
catch	→	capture, grab, seize
change	→	alter, switch, vary
children	→	kids, tots, youngsters
clean	→	launder, scrub, wash
close	→	fasten, seal, shut
cold	→	chilly, frosty, icy
come	→	approach, arrive, reach
cook	→	bake, broil, fry, roast
crooked	→	bent, curved, twisted
cry	→	bawl, sob, wail, weep
cut	→	chop, clip, sever, snip
cute	→	attractive, darling, pretty

3

dangerous	→	hazardous, risky, unsafe
dark	→	dismal, gloomy, shadowy
destroy	→	demolish, ruin, wreck
different	→	distinct, unique, varied
dig	→	excavate, scoop
dirty	→	filthy, soiled
do	→	accomplish, achieve, finish
done	→	completed, concluded, ended, finished
draw	→	picture, portray, sketch
dream	→	fantasize, imagine
eager	→	anxious, enthusiastic, interested
eat	→	devour, dine, feast, taste
end	→	cease, complete, finish, terminate, quit
enjoy	→	appreciate, like, relish, savor
enough	→	ample, plenty, sufficient
excited	→	eager, enthusiastic, interested
fair	→	honest, impartial, just
fair	→	bazaar, carnival, festival

famous	→	celebrated, popular, renowned, well-known
far	→	distant, remote, removed
fast	→	hasty, quick, rapid, speedy, swift
fat	→	chubby, heavy, plump, stout
fight	→	battle, dispute, feud, struggle
fill	→	load, pack, stuff
find	→	discover, locate, retrieve, uncover
fine	→	excellent, good, splendid
fix	→	adjust, mend, repair
flat	→	even, level, smooth
fly	→	flee, glide, soar
frighten	→	alarm, scare, terrify
full	→	crowded, loaded, packed, stuffed
funny	→	amusing, comical, humorous, silly
garbage	→	junk, rubbish, trash, waste
get	→	acquire, collect, fetch, obtain, secure
give	→	grant, present, provide, supply
go	→	depart, leave, move, proceed
good	→	appropriate, fine, suitable

3

great	→	glorious, magnificent, splendid, terrific, wonderful
grow	→	cultivate, plant, raise
happy	→	cheerful, contented, delighted, joyful, pleased
hard	→	firm, rigid, solid, stiff
hard	→	difficult, tough, troublesome
hate	→	detest, dislike, loathe
have	→	hold, own, possess
help	→	aid, assist, support
hide	→	camouflage, conceal, cover, mask
high	→	lofty, tall, towering
hit	→	slap, slug, smack, strike, swat
hold	→	grab, grasp, grip
hot	→	sizzling, steaming, sweltering
house	→	dwelling, home, residence, shelter
hurry	→	dash, hasten, hustle, rush, speed
hurt	→	damage, harm, injure, wound
idea	→	concept, notion, thought, plan

important	→	meaningful, necessary, significant, vital
interesting	→	absorbing, captivating, fascinating
jump	→	hop, leap, spring
keep	→	hold, retain, save
kill	→	assassinate, execute, slay
kind	→	considerate, helpful, thoughtful
laugh	→	chuckle, giggle
lift	→	boost, hoist, raise
like	→	admire, appreciate, enjoy
little	→	minute, slight, tiny, small, wee
long	→	drawn-out, lengthy
look	→	gaze, glance, stare
love	→	adore, cherish, treasure, worship
mad	→	angry, annoyed, cross, enraged, furious, irritated
make	→	build, construct, create, design, invent, manufacture
many	→	numerous, several, various
mark	→	label, sign, stamp, tap

3

mean	→	cross, irritable, malicious, unkind
move	→	amble, crawl, hobble, plod, saunter, scamper, shuffle
neat	→	orderly, tidy, well-kept
need	→	lack, require, want
new	→	current, fresh, modern, original, recent
nice	→	agreeable, fine, good, pleasant
night	→	dark, evening
often	→	frequently, repeatedly
old	→	aged, ancient, archaic, elderly, feeble, frail, worn
open	→	begin, establish, start, unlock, unseal
part	→	piece, portion, share, section
people	→	folks, individuals, public
pick	→	choose, elect, select
picture	→	drawing, illustration, photo, representation
place	→	area, location, site, space,
play	→	frolic, romp
pretty	→	attractive, beautiful, good-looking, handsome, lovely

pull	→	drag, haul, tug, tow, yank
push	→	nudge, press, shove, thrust
put	→	arrange, lay, place, set
quiet	→	calm, peaceful, restful, silent, still, tranquil
rich	→	affluent, prosperous, wealthy
right	→	accurate, correct, factual, proper, true
rough	→	bumpy, choppy, coarse, uneven
run	→	dash, hasten, hurry, jog, race, sprint
sad	→	blue, depressed, forlorn, gloomy, unhappy
say	→	comment, declare, exclaim
scared	→	afraid, alarmed, frightened, startled, terrified
sea	→	ocean, waters
see	→	gaze, peek, spot, stare, watch
shine	→	glimmer, glisten, sparkle, twinkle
show	→	demonstrate, display, exhibit, present, reveal
sleep	→	doze, nap, slumber, snooze
slide	→	coast, glide, skid, slip

3

slow	→	behind, delaying, sluggish, unhurried
smart	→	bright, clever, intelligent, wise
smell	→	aroma, fragrance, odor, scent
smooth	→	even, glassy, polished, sleek
sound	→	bang, crash, roar
start	→	begin, commence, launch
stir	→	blend, combine, mix, scramble
stop	→	cease, discontinue, end, finish, halt, quit
store	→	market, shop
store	→	save
storm	→	blizzard, gale, hurricane, tornado
story	→	account, legend, narrative, tale
strange	→	bizarre, odd, peculiar, unfamiliar, weird
stream	→	brook, creek
street	→	avenue, road
strong	→	mighty, muscular, powerful, sturdy
take	→	capture, grab, obtain, seize
talk	→	converse, discuss, speak
tell	→	explain, narrate, report, recite, state

thin	→	lean, skinny, slender, slim
think	→	believe, consider, guess, imagine, reflect, wonder
throw	→	cast, fling, hurl, pitch, toss
tie	→	bind, fasten, secure, wrap
tight	→	firm, snug
trick	→	deceive, fool, mislead
trip	→	excursion, journey, tour, stumble
trouble	→	bother, difficulty, inconvenience, worry
true	→	pivot, rotate, spin, twirl, twist, wind
ugly	→	gruesome, hideous, homely, unattractive
walk	→	march, saunter, stroll
want	→	crave, desire
wide	→	broad, expansive
wonderful	→	glorious, great, marvelous, spectacular, splendid
work	→	labor, toil
world	→	earth, glove, universe
write	→	draft, record
wrong	→	faulty, incorrect, mistaken

3

Spelling Rules

The spelling rules listed below hold true more than 80 percent of the time.

1. **Q** is followed by **u**.

   quiet

2. No English word ends in **v**.

   love

3. Capitalize proper nouns.

   America

4. Plurals: Words ending in **x, s, ss, sh, ch**, add **es**.

   dress—dresses

   Words ending in a single f, change f to v and add **es**.

   shelf—shelves

5. Apostrophes: Show omitted letters in contractions.

   do not—don't

   Indicate possessive forms of nouns.

   boy's **hat**

4

6. Usually, i comes before e,

   believe

   except after c,

   receive

   or when sounded like a,

   neighbor.

7. Suffixes: Words ending in e, drop the e if suffix begins with a vowel.

   bake—baking

   Keep the e if suffix begins with a consonant.

   manage—management

   Words ending in y (following a consonant), change y to i unless suffix begins with i.

   fly—flies—flying

   Words ending in a single consonant (following a single vowel), double the final consonant before adding ed or ing.

   ship—shipped—shipping

Grammar and Sentences

Grammar rules are the rules for how to put ideas together in writing. Grammar also gives labels to certain kinds of words.

Adjectives

An adjective is a word that describes a noun. Adjectives describe nouns by telling what something looks, feels, tastes, sounds, or smells like. Adjectives can describe feelings. Adjectives can also tell how many.

> She has a blue bike.

> The boy was happy.

> There are ten cookies left.

> I just have a few books.

5

Adjectives that compare

Add **er** to most adjectives when comparing two things.

> Frog is bigger than Toad.

Add **est** to most adjectives when comparing more than two things.

> She is the tallest girl in the class.

Nouns

A noun is a word that names a person, place, or thing.

> girl   school   book

A noun can name more than one person, place or thing. Often an *s* is added to nouns to make them mean more than one.

> dog—dogs bike—bikes store—stores

Nouns that are special

Special nouns begin with capital letters.

Days of the week are special nouns.

> Sunday Tuesday Thursday

Names of cities, states, and streets are special nouns.

> Denver, Colorado Riverside Drive

Names of holidays are special nouns.

> Thanksgiving Labor Day

Names of the months are special nouns.

> March July September

Names of people are special nouns.

> Joe Denny Pam Little

Titles of people are special nouns.

> Mr. Weber Mrs. Lopez Dr. Bell

Pronouns

A pronoun is a word that takes the place of one or more nouns. Pronouns are words like I, he, she, we, it, and they. Pronouns are used in the naming part of a sentence.

Sam ate the apple.

He ate the apple.

Pronouns that are special

The pronouns **I** and **me** are names you call yourself.

Use **I** at the beginning of a sentence.

I will sit down.

Use **I** when you talk about yourself and a friend. Name yourself last.

Ben and I like to sing.

Use **me** at the end of a sentence.

Jenny plays with me.

Use **me** after an action verb.

She makes me laugh.

The teacher tells Sally and me to be quiet.

5

Sentences

A sentence is a group of words that tells a complete thought.

A sentence begins with a capital letter and ends with a punctuation mark.

Frog wrote Toad a letter.

There are two parts to a sentence. The naming part tells who or what the sentence is about and the action part tells something about the naming part. The two parts make a complete thought.

Naming Part	Action Part
Frog	wrote Toad a letter.

Kinds of sentences

There are three kinds of sentences.

A statement is a sentence that tells something. It always begins with a capital letter and ends with a period (.).

Frog and Toad are friends.

A question is a sentence that asks something. It always begins with a capital letter and ends with a question mark (?).

What does the lost button look like?

An exclamation is a sentence that shows strong feeling. It always begins with a capital letter and ends with an exclamation mark (!).

I found the button!

Verbs

A verb is a word that shows action.

Ameleia Bedelia draws the drapes.

Frog and Toad walked down the path.

Now action verbs

Add **s** to an action verb that tells what one person or thing does now.

Toad waits by the mailbox for a letter.

Frog writes a letter to Toad.

5

Past action verbs

Add **ed** to an action verb that tells what happened in the past.

Frog walked to the river.

Toad looked for his button.

Some action verbs do not add ed to tell what happened in the past.

He runs fast. (now)

He ran fast. (past)

Now	Past
come, comes	came
go, goes	went
run, runs	ran
take	took

Verbs that do not show action

Some verbs do not show action. These verbs can tell about now, the present, or the past.

Frog is nice to Toad. (now)

Frog was nice to Toad. (past)

Now	Past
am, is	was
are	were

Use am or was with the word I.

I am seven years old. (now)

I was late for school. (past)

Use is or was with one person or thing.

> The girl is **sad. (now)**

> The cat was **lost. (past)**

Use are or were with more than one person or thing.

> The boys are **tired. (now)**

> The stores were **closed. (past)**

Other verbs that do not show action are have, has, and had. These verbs tell about things that belong to someone or something.

> Toad has a cold. **(now)**

> Toad had a cold. **(past)**

Now	Past
has, have	had

Use have or had with the word I.

> I have **a new bike. (now)**

> I had **a good lunch. (past)**

Use has or had with one person or thing.

The girl has **a little puppy. (now)**

The book had **many pages. (past)**

Use have or had with more than one person or thing.

We have **a new house. (now)**

We had **a good time. (past)**

Mechanics

Capital Letters

Capital letters are used to show that a word is special. The rules below tell how to use capital letters.

sentences   Capitalize the first word in a sentence.

This book is very funny.

names   Capitalize the first and last name of a person.

Kelly Nelson   Tom Johnson

title   Capitalize the titles of a person.

Mr. Rogers   Mrs. Davis   Dr. Smith

I   Capitalize the word I.

She and I will walk to the park.

streets   Capitalize the name of a street.

321 Lakeside St.   98 Pine Dr.

654 Second Ave.

places   Capitalize the names of cities and states.

Seattle, Washington   Orlando, Florida

days   Capitalize days of the week.

Monday   Wednesday   Friday

6

months	Capitalize months of the year.
	January April July October
holidays	Capitalize the important words in holidays.
	Valentine's Day Fourth of July
titles	Capitalize the important words in the title of a book.
	Amelia Bedelia Goes Camping
	Frog and Toad All Year

Punctuation Marks

Punctuation marks are used to add meaning to sentences and to separate ideas. The rules below tell how to use punctuation marks.

Apostrophe

contraction   An apostrophe (') i's used to show that one or more letters have been taken out to form a contraction.

does not   doesn't   I am   I'm

Colon

time   A colon (:) is placed between the hour and the minutes when writing the time of day in numerals.

9:00 A.M.   5:30 P. M.

6

Comma

address   A comma (,) is used between a city and a state and between a city and a country.

Little Rock, Arkansas (city, state)

Paris, France (city, country)

date	A comma (,) is used between the day and the year.
	March 16, 1992 December 6, 1999
greeting/ closing	A comma (,) is used after the greeting and the closing of a friendly letter.
	Dear Grandma, Sincerely,
list	A comma (,) is used to separate a list of words.
	The store sold grapes, apples, and peaches.

Exclamation mark

An exclamation mark (!) is used at the end of an exclamation. An exclamation is a sentence that shows surprise or strong feeling.

I can't believe it!

Period

abbreviation

A period (.) is used after an abbreviation.

Doctor Jackson—Dr. Jackson

inch—in.

Do not use periods after United States Postal Service abbreviations for states.

California—CA   Iowa—IA

initials

A period (.) is used after initials that stand for names.

Jane M. Sable   Robert J. Rose

sentence

A period (.) is used at the end of a sentence that is a statement or a command.

She is going to visit the zoo.

Open the door.

6

Question mark

A question mark (?) is used at the end of a question. A question is a sentence that asks something.

Did you find the piece of paper?

Quotation marks

conversation

Quotation marks (" ") are used before and after a sentence or paragraph to show when someone is speaking.

My brother said, "I have an apple in my lunch."

Underlines

title

A title of a book is underlined.

<u>Frog and Toad Are Friends</u>

 # Forms of Writing

Paragraph

A paragraph is a group of sentences that tells about one idea called the main idea. The sentence that tells the main idea is called the topic sentence. Usually, it is the first sentence in the paragraph. The other sentences in the paragraph that describe the main idea are called the supporting sentences.

The first line of a paragraph must be indented. This means that the first word is a few spaces from the left margin. The second line of the paragraph begins at the left margin.

Example:

During the summer, my family and I like to spend most of our time at the cabin. On really hot days, we jump off the dock and swim in the water. On cloudy days, we take short hikes or go fishing. In the evenings, we build a campfire and roast marshmallows. Sometimes, if the night sky is clear, we count the falling stars. Our cabin is where you will find us during the summer.

7

Friendly Letter

A friendly letter is a letter that you write to someone you know. When you write a friendly letter, you can share ideas or tell about something you have done. You can also write a friendly letter to say thank you or to invite someone to a special activity. There are five parts in a friendly letter. They are: the heading, the greeting, the body, the closing, and the signature.

Example:

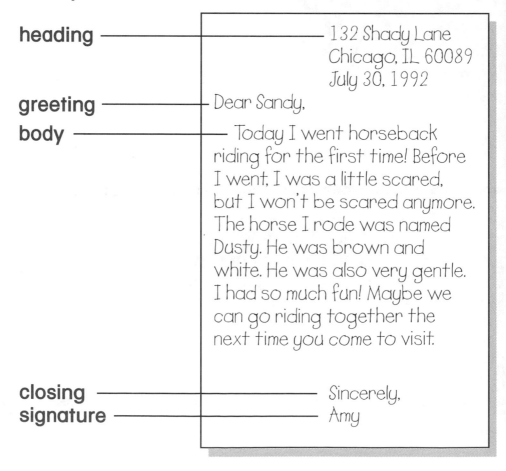

heading — 132 Shady Lane
Chicago, IL 60089
July 30, 1992

greeting — Dear Sandy,

body — Today I went horseback riding for the first time! Before I went, I was a little scared, but I won't be scared anymore. The horse I rode was named Dusty. He was brown and white. He was also very gentle. I had so much fun! Maybe we can go riding together the next time you come to visit.

closing — Sincerely,
signature — Amy

Envelope

An envelope is used to send a letter. The mailing address tells who is receiving the letter. The return address tells who is sending the letter. Before a letter can be mailed, a stamp is needed in the upper right hand corner of the envelope.

return address

mailing address

stamp

Amy Learner
132 Shady Ln.
Chicago, IL 60603

Sandy Brighton
465 Tulip Ln.
Nashville, TN 37203

U.S. Postage

7

Narrative Writing

Narrative writing tells a real or imaginary story about something that has happened. Narrative writing tells about one or more characters and where the story takes place. The events within the story are told in the sequence in which they happened. This sequence of events gives the story a beginning, middle, and end.

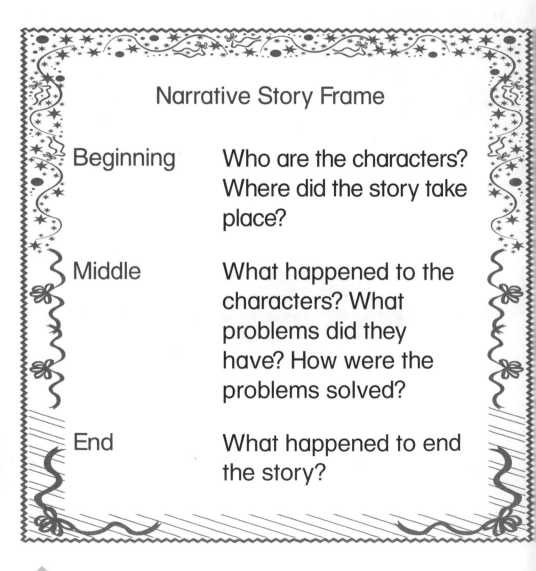

Narrative Story Frame

Beginning

Who are the characters? Where did the story take place?

Middle

What happened to the characters? What problems did they have? How were the problems solved?

End

What happened to end the story?

Example:

> Whenever I go to the beach, I find so many fun things to do. First, I run along the water's edge and play tag with the waves. Next, I lay on the hot sand and listen to the screeching seagulls. When I decide to cool off, I jump and run into the waves. Finally, I walk along the beach looking for shells. I always enjoy my day at the beach!

Descriptive Writing

Descriptive writing creates a picture in the reader's mind. Descriptive writing uses sensory words about how something looks, tastes, smells, sounds, or how it feels to touch. Descriptive writing also may tell how the writer feels about the person or thing being described. In a piece of descriptive writing, the paragraphs either begin or end with a topic sentence. The topic sentence tells the reader what the paragraph is about.

Descriptive Paragraph Frame

Topic sentence

What is the paragraph going to be about?

7

Supporting sentences

What words describe the person or thing?
How does something look?

Taste?
Smell?
Sound?
Feel?

How does it make the writer feel?
(Happy, sad, scared, excited, angry)

Topic sentence

What was the paragraph about?

Example:

A storm warns you when it's on its way. The sky fills with dark, gray clouds. Thunder begins to rumble softly. The air smells damp and moist. The trees rustle and the wind blows though their leaves. Far away bright lightning flashes.

Poem

A poem is a special way to tell about an idea you have, the way you feel, or to tell a story. A poem uses a few words to describe something or to tell about your own or someone else's feelings. Sometimes, poems have rhyming words. Most poems have a pattern of beats called rhythm.

Examples:

I can always find a patch of blue sky, a raindrop, a teardrop, or a satisfied sigh.

But I can't always find a mountain-top view, a rainbow, a halo, or a friend such as you.

Timid, young firefly
Feeling brave; flashes—light on!
Courage gone—light off!

Kinds of Writing

There are many different kinds of writing. Listed below are some of the different kinds.

Fantasy

Fantasies are stories that cannot really happen. In a fantasy, people may do things that real people cannot do. For example, people may fly, go back in time, or turn into something else. The animals in a fantasy may act, talk, and think like people. Some fantasy have a mix of events, some that cannot happen and some that can.

Fiction

Fiction stories tell about people and things that are not real. These stories are made up. However, they seem very real. The characters, the places, the events, and the endings can be written as though they really happened. Listed below are some examples of different kinds of fiction.

Historical Fiction

Historical fiction tells how people lived at a particular time. Everything that the characters say and do must match the time and place of the story.

Humorous Fiction

Humorous fiction is for enjoyment and usually very funny. The author often likes to stretch the reader's imagination as he describes the characters and the events of the story.

Realistic Fiction

Realistic fiction seems very real but is not. The characters, the places, the events, and the endings can be written as though they really happened.

Science Fiction

Science fiction tells about adventures that happen in such places as outer space, other planets, and the world of the future.

Folklore

Folklore are stories that were retold over and over long before they were ever written down. Folklore often begins with "Once upon a time" or "Long, long ago." The story usually ends with " . . . and they all lived happily ever after." The characters are generally good and bad, pretty and ugly, wise and foolish, or brave and timid. Magic is a part of folklore. Folklore also stresses such values as loyalty, honesty, and courage. Some examples of folklore are fables, fairytales, and folktales.

Fables

Fables are short stories that were made up long ago. Most of the characters are animals that act, talk, and think like people. One of the animals learns a lesson at the end of the fable. The lesson learned is called a moral.

Fairy Tales

The characters in fairy tales are usually kings, queens, a princess, a prince, fairies, a wicked

7

stepmother, elves, and other imaginary beings with magical powers.

Folktales

Folktales are stories that were made up long ago. These stories were to tell how something came to be or to teach something. The characters in folktales may be people or animals or both. The people in folktales are often very silly. The animals in folktales usually act, talk, and think like people. Folktales are usually made up of happenings in threes.

Historical Writing

Historical writing tells about the life of people, a country, or a specific event in history. An example of historical writing is a biography.

Biography

A biography tells about the life of a real person. This person may have lived in the past or may be living now. Usually, this person has done something very interesting or important. A biography is written by a person that the story is not about.

Mystery

A mystery is a secret or something that is unexplained. In a mystery, the character or characters find out what the secret is or discover the explanation. The author gives the reader clues so that the reader can solve the mystery along with the characters. A mystery is usually full of action, suspense, and surprise.

Nonfiction/Factual

Nonfiction stories tell about real people, places, and things. These stories are true. The information an author includes in a nonfiction story is factual and up-to-date.

Poetry

Poems are sets of words that are short and songlike. Poems can have rhyming words, tell a story, or describe a feeling. Poems can be about anything. Writing poetry is like painting a picture with words. A poem can help the author and the reader see something in a new way. Poems can be easy to remember as well as fun to say out loud.

7

Organizing Ideas for Writing and Studying

You can organize your writing in many different ways.

Character Map

A character map helps you see the relationships between the characters in a story.

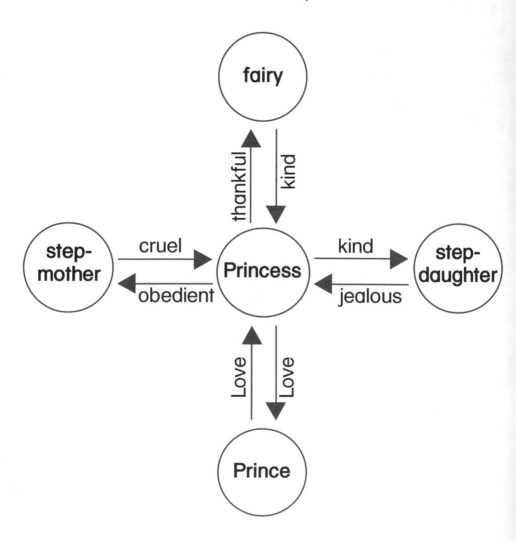

Contrast diagram or Venn diagram

You can use a contrast or Venn diagram to show how two characters or ideas are alike as well as different.

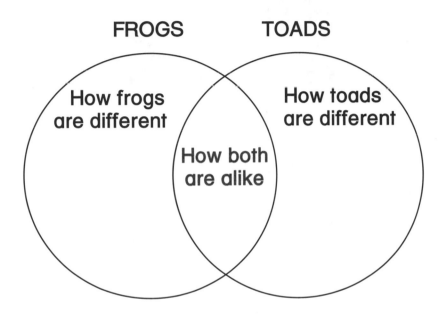

FROGS   TOADS

How frogs
are different

How toads
are different

How both
are alike

7

Drawing

Draw pictures on paper to help you get ideas to write about.

Journal Writing

Look through your journal. Choose an idea or topic you have written about and turn it into an interesting story.

Number Outlining

Number outlining is a way to organize information when writing or studying. The number I shows the main idea. The number 2 shows the supporting details.

I Three foods I like to eat:

  2 pizza

  2 apples

  2 ice cream

7

Opinion-Proof

An opinion-proof helps you to form an opinion and to support it. Opinion-proof notes can also become a paragraph. The opinion becomes the main idea and the proofs become the supporting sentences.

Opinion	Proof
My grandpa is lots of fun.	He takes me to football games. We go fishing together.

My Grandpa

My grandpa is a lot of fun. He takes me to football games on weekends. Sometimes we go fishing together. I like spending time with my grandpa. He's great!

Problem/Solution

The problem becomes the main idea. The solutions become the supporting details. This is another way of organizing information.

Problem	Solution
Toad can't think of a story.	1. He walks up and down the front porch.
	2. He stands on his head.
	3. He pours a glass of water over his head.
	4. He bangs his head on the wall.

Sequence Chart

Sometimes it is helpful to draw or write down the events in the order that they happen in a story.

 MY BALLOON

One day my best friend gave me a balloon.

I really like balloons.

I started running with my balloon. It followed me everywhere.

I tripped and fell.

I no longer had hold of my balloon.

My friend just happened to have another one.

Story Frame or Story Plan

Sometimes it helps to use a story frame or story plan to organize your ideas for writing. You can fill in the frame or plan and have an outline for your story.

Story Plan

_____ _____

Name　　　　　　　Story Title

Character(s):	Setting:
_____	_____
character	The story takes place
_____	_____
describe	Illustrate below
_____	↓
describe	
_____	
character	
_____	
describe	
_____	
describe	

Problem: _____

_____

_____

_____

Solution: _____

_____

_____

Story Frame

Setting (where)

_____

Characters (who)

_____

The Problem (what)

_____

Events

1. _____

2. _____

3. _____

End (How the problem gets solved)

_____

_____

_____

_____

_____

_____

7

111

Two-Column Notes

Two-column notes help writers organize main ideas and details. The questions or key words on the left are the main points. The answers on the right are the supporting details.

Setting:	Toad's front porch.
Characters:	Frog
	Toad
	Snail
Problem:	Toad is sad because he never gets any mail.
Solution:	Frog writes Toad a letter.

Webbing/Mapping

Use a web or map to write down important information.

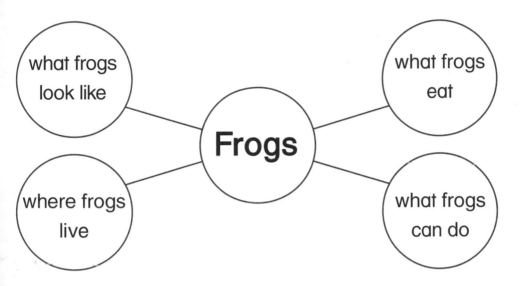

Process Writing

Process Writing helps you improve your writing skills.

The Process Writing Steps

1. Prewriting
2. First Draft
3. Revision
   - self evaluation
   - peer conference
4. Self Editing
5. Assisted Editing
6. Final Draft
7. Publishing/Sharing

Prewriting

Prewriting is a step that helps you decide what it is you wish to write about.

Write down all your ideas or topics. Pick one idea to use for a story. Circle the idea or topic you want to write about.

my birthday	friends	my cat
(pets)	my bike	baseball

Then write your circled idea down. List words for your story.

<u>Pets</u>

dogs	fluffy
my puppy	Shep
brown	kitten
white	sleepy

Look under the section "Organizing Ideas for Writing and Studying" (p. 102) for other ways to plan your ideas when writing.

First Draft

Write your story. Look at your prewriting for ideas.

My pets

I have two pets. One is a cat, and one is a dog. The cat is ...

Revision

- **self-evaluation**
  Read your first draft. Read each word. What can you do to make it better?

  > Do you have a beginning, middle, and end to your story?

  > Do all the words make sense?

  > Do you need to change anything?

- **peer-conferencing**
  Ask a friend to read or listen to your story. Does your friend have any suggestions to make your story better?

  You might want to use Editor's Marks to mark the part to be fixed.

EDITOR'S MARKS

≡ capitalize

∧ add something

⸺ℓ take out something

⬭ spell correctly

o end mark

／ make lowercase

⁋ paragraph

Final Draft

Make any changes in your story. Recopy it. Use your best handwriting.

Proofreading

Use this Writer's Checklist to help with proofreading.

- **Did I put my name on my paper?**

- **Did I use capitals?**

- **Did I use the endmarks (.) (?) and (!)?**

- **Did I check my spelling?**

Publishing/Sharing

To publish your story you need all the parts of a book. Make the parts of your book.

Title Page

The title page tells three things:

1. The book title

2. The author—who wrote the book

3. The illustrator—who drew the pictures

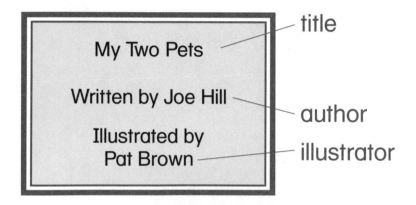

My Two Pets — title

Written by Joe Hill — author

Illustrated by
Pat Brown — illustrator

Copyright Date

The copyright date is usually on the back side of the title page. Copyright means that only the author can copy or sell the book. The copyright symbol looks like this: ©. You can also see the year the book was published and the name of the publisher.

Copyright © 2000 by Kendall/Hunt Publishing Co.

Dedication Page

Sometimes the author writes a book for someone special. The person's name will be on the dedication page. (The author can dedicate the book to more than one person.)

for Jan and Bob

Table of Contents

The table of contents tells the titles of the chapters and the page numbers where the chapters begin.

CONTENTS

About The Author/Illustrator

This page tells the reader about the author's real life. It also can tell about the illustrator.

About the Author

Joe is seven years old. He is in second grade at Shiloh Elementary School. He lives with his mom and two brothers in New York City.

Joe wants to be a teacher when he grows up.

Sharing

When your writing is finished, share your story with friends, class, or family.

Index

as special nouns, 80
in stories. *See* Characters
Period (.), 91
    with abbreviation, 35–36, 48–49, 91
    at end of sentence, 82
    with initials, 91
    with sentence, 91
Places
    capital letter with, 87
    in realistic fiction, 101
    in science fiction, 101
Plurals, spelling rules for, 77
Poem, 99, 103
Prefix
    defined, 63
    word division with, 61
Prewriting, 115–116
Problem/solution, 109
Process writing, 115–122
    final draft, 119
    first draft, 117
    prewriting, 115–116
    proofreading, 119
    publishing, 120–122
    revision, 118
    sharing, 122
Pronouns
    defined, 81
    special, 81
Proofreading, 119
Proper nouns, 77
Publishing
    About the Author/Illustrator, 122
    copyright date, 120
    dedication page, 121
    table of contents, 121
    title page, 120
Punctuation marks
    apostrophe ('), 45, 77, 89
    colon (:), 89
    comma (,), 89–90

exclamation mark (!), 83, 90
period (.), 91. See *also* Period
question mark (?), 82, 92
quotation marks (""), 92
in sentence, 82, 91
underline (_), 92
P words, 20–21

Question mark (?), 82, 92
Question, 82
    in two-column notes, 112
Quotation marks (""), 92
Q words, 22

Realistic fiction, 101
Return address, 95
Revision, 118
Rhyming words, 99, 103
Rhythm, in poem, 99
R words, 23

Science fiction, 101
Self-evaluation, 118
Sentences
    capital letters in, 87
    defined, 82
    exclamation, 90
    kinds of, 82–83
    in paragraph, 93
    period with, 82, 91
    question, 92
    supporting, 93, 98
    topic, 93, 97–98
Sequence chart, 110
Sharing, 122
Signal words, 57
Signature, of friendly letter, 94
Spelling rules, 77–78
Stamp, 95
State abbreviations, 58–60
Statement, 82
States, 58–60
Story